What Leaders Are Saying

. . . allowed me to ... make it personal
and focus my observations and prayers.

. . . took it from theory to practical.

A chance to contemplate and really stop to think.

. . . helped in our understanding and application for our ministry.

It made me think about how to apply this to my community, my church, my ladies.

. . . something you will use for your ministry team.

. . . helps complete the thinking/learning process.

I had several aha moments.

. . . an eye-opener in so many aspects.

Companion Workbook with Bonus Chapter

ReTHINKING WOMEN'S MINISTRY Workbook

Cyndee Ownbey

Rethinking Women's Ministry Workbook

Published by ONB Press

www.womensministrytoolbox.com

Cover and interior design by Michelle Rayburn www.missionandmedia.com.

Copy edit by Michelle Rayburn.

ISBN-13: 978-1-7334710-1-5

Printed in the United States of America

Dedication

To the women's ministry leaders who lovingly and faithfully serve the women in their churches and communities

Contents

SECTION 2: *Bonus Chapter and Worksheets*

SECTION 3: *Summarize*

SECTION 4: *Bonus Resources*

How to Use This Workbook

The *Rethinking Women's Ministry Workbook* is designed to be read alongside the book *Rethinking Women's Ministry: Biblical, Practical Tools for Cultivating a Flourishing Community.*

The following pages contain questions, exercises, and bonus materials that invite women's ministry leaders to dig deeper and apply the information from each chapter of *Rethinking Women's Ministry.*

While you are welcome to dive in and proceed at your own pace, there is a ten-week reading plan that you may find helpful. You may also decide to read the book and workbook together as a team or use it in one of these ways:

- Discuss the book during a weekend leadership retreat.
- Focus on a handful of chapters during an all-day meeting.
- Discuss portions of the book at your regular team meetings each month.

It's unlikely your women's ministry needs a complete overhaul. In fact, you're no doubt doing a lot of things really well and blessing each woman who attends. I pray you'll be open to how a few small changes might extend the reach of your ministry and accelerate the spiritual growth of the women in your church. It isn't necessarily a matter of doing more but determining if there's a better, more effective way.

I pray God will guide you as you read these pages. I pray He'll make clear what your team should keep doing, what needs to be refined, and what needs to be removed so the women you serve may grow in their love for one another and for Christ.

For additional support, please visit **www.womensministrytoolbox.com** and join with other leaders in the closed Facebook group, Women's Ministry Toolbox Community.

May we rise to the challenge of cultivating communities that flourish,

Cyndee

10-Week Reading Plan

Read the following chapters each week in *Rethinking Women's Ministry: Biblical, Practical Tools for Cultivating a Flourishing Community.*

Week 1 – Intro, Chapter 1 & 2

Week 2 – Chapter 3

Week 3 – Chapter 4 & 5

Week 4 – Chapters 6

Week 5 – Chapter 7

Week 6 – Chapter 8

Week 7 – Chapter 9

Week 8 – Chapter 10 & 11

Week 9 – Chapter 12

Week 10 – Chapter 13, 14, & Bonus Chapter (in the workbook)

SECTION 1

Introduction Questions

1. Which age group(s) do you find missing from many of your women's ministry events and activities? If it varies by event and activity, consider making a list.

2. Do you have a women's ministry purpose statement or mission statement? If yes, write it below. If not, what two or three things do you think it should include?

3. **Team task:** Create or revisit your women's ministry mission statement. For help, see womensministrytoolbox.com/mission-statement.

Chapter 1

Who Are We Trying to Reach?

1. Read and record **MATTHEW 28:19–20**.

2. Does your team struggle to reach millennials and Gen Z women?

   ☐ yes ☐ no ☐ not sure

3. Which generalizations about millennials and Gen Z surprised you?

4. What **needs** may millennial and Gen Z women have that your women's ministry could meet?

5. List five things your team could start doing to better connect with millennial and Gen Z women.

6. Which barriers to participation (work, spiritual apathy, biblical illiteracy, family, cliques, and cultural) do you see reflected in your church and community? List at least two examples.

7. What did you find most challenging or convicting in chapter 1 of *Rethinking Women's Ministry*?

Keep a Record

Much like the Prayer Points and Action Items in *Rethinking Women's Ministry,* you'll find a Keep a Record section after each set of chapter questions in this workbook. Keeping a record provides a place for you to record key information:

1. Prayer requests and answers
2. Action items and their outcomes

Commit to taking the next step. Record how God answers your prayers. Make a note of the outcome when you've stepped obediently forward in faith.

I pray that you and your team will be able to see God at work!

Keep a Record

Prayer Requests	PRAYER REQUESTS	BEGAN PRAYING (DATE)	HOW GOD ANSWERED

Action Items	ACTION ITEMS	DATE TO IMPLEMENT	OUTCOME

Chapter 2

Impact of Social Media and the Internet

1. Read and record **JAMES 1:5** and **1 CORINTHIANS 10:23**.

2. Do you find that your ministry is in competition with online ministries, online Bible studies, or devotional apps? If so, how?

3. Which of the seven reasons for why women are leaving the physical church for online ministry do you think may be an issue in your church? (See pages 24–27 in *Rethinking Women's Ministry.*) How can you address them?

4. If God brought a particular woman to mind as you read through the seven reasons, please take a few moments to pray for her now. You may wish to write out your prayer below.

5. Which of the four internet traps can you relate to, and how? (See page 28 in *Rethinking Women's Ministry.*)

6. Record at least one thing you can do to avoid the four internet traps.

7. To what do you sense God is drawing your attention in chapter 2 of *Rethinking Women's Ministry*?

Keep a Record

Prayer Requests	PRAYER REQUESTS	BEGAN PRAYING (DATE)	HOW GOD ANSWERED

Action Items	ACTION ITEMS	DATE TO IMPLEMENT	OUTCOME

Chapter 3

Community and Cliques

1. Read and record **HEBREWS 10:24–25** and **1 PETER 3:8**.

2. To what degree are cliques an issue in your church? Record at least one example of a clique in your women's ministry.

3. Seek and find! Find an icebreaker that encourages community and connection to use at one of your next events. Pinterest and the icebreaker games on the Women's Ministry Toolbox site are great places to start. Note the icebreaker you would like to try below.

4. What is one thing new you could do to encourage community at your next women's ministry event or activity?

5. What is your process for welcoming first-time guests? If there isn't one in place, what are some things you think it should include?

6. Write a prayer for growing community among the women in your church.

Keep a Record

Prayer Requests

PRAYER REQUESTS	BEGAN PRAYING (DATE)	HOW GOD ANSWERED

Action Items

ACTION ITEMS	DATE TO IMPLEMENT	OUTCOME

31 Introduction Icebreaker Questions

HOW TO USE: The next time you instruct a group to introduce themselves, ask each person to share their name and the answer to one of the questions below (you select the question ahead of time). Some people will appreciate having the question written on the board before the request is made, as it gives them time to think through their response. Either way, give them time to think by answering the question yourself first and then asking for a volunteer to go next.

31 Great Icebreaker Questions for Introductions

1. If money were no object, what would you do with your life?
2. What is one of your pet peeves?
3. If you could host a talk show, who would be your first guest?
4. What are you most passionate about?
5. What is your favorite thing to spend money on?
6. What is your favorite color, and how does that color make you feel?
7. Which household chore do you dread the most?
8. What is your favorite time of day and why?
9. What is one of your favorite movies, and which character in the movie is most like you?
10. What are three of your favorite foods?
11. What is your favorite outdoor activity?
12. If finances and time were not an object, what hobby would you adopt and why?
13. What is a favorite memory you have from high school?
14. What was your favorite class in school and why?
15. Share one thing that you love to do that you get to do nearly every day.

16. What is one important skill every person should master?
17. What is your favorite local restaurant and the meal you most enjoy eating when there?
18. If you could live in any sitcom, which one would it be?
19. How would you spend one million dollars?
20. Name two things you consider yourself to be exceptionally good at.
21. What is the best dessert you've ever had?
22. What are your three favorite smells?
23. If you were in the Miss America talent competition, what would your talent be?
24. If you had one extra hour of free time per day, how would you use it?
25. When was the last time you did something for the first time? What was it?
26. If you could be anywhere doing anything right now, where would you be, and what would you be doing?
27. If you joined the circus, what act would you most want to perform?
28. Which aspect of your daily routine do you look forward to the most?
29. What is your favorite day of the year?
30. What is something you have that is of sentimental value?
31. What one thing (modern convenience) could you not live without?

Chapter 4

Rethinking Teams

1. Read and record **PROVERBS 15:22** and **EPHESIANS 4:16**.

2. Pray and ask God to help you honestly answer the following questions about your leadership style.

   Would others consider you to be a team player?

   ☐ No ☐ Somewhat ☐ Definitely ☐ Not sure

   Do you delegate?

   ☐ No ☐ Sometimes ☐ Definitely ☐ Not sure

   Do you let others lead?

   ☐ No ☐ Sometimes ☐ Definitely ☐ Not sure

   Are you willing to lead?

   ☐ No ☐ Somewhat ☐ Definitely ☐ Not sure

3. Circle any answer in question number 2 that may be impacting your ability to lead. Spend some time in prayer seeking how God may want you to lead differently.

4. Read through the Bible passage below. Circle each occurrence of the word "body." Underline every occurrence of the word "part" and every named body part.

> If the whole body were an eye, where would the sense of hearing be? If the whole body were an ear, where would the sense of smell be? But in fact God has placed the parts in the body, every one of them, just as he wanted them to be. If they were all one part, where would the body be? As it is, there are many parts, but one body. The eye cannot say to the hand, "I don't need you!" And the head cannot say to the feet, "I don't need you!" On the contrary, those parts of the body that seem to be weaker are indispensable, and the parts that we think are less honorable we treat with special honor. And the parts that are unpresentable are treated with special modesty, while our presentable parts need no special treatment. But God has put the body together, giving greater honor to the parts that lacked it, so that there should be no division in the body, but that its parts should have equal concern for each other. If one part suffers, every part suffers with it; if one part is honored, every part rejoices with it. (1 Corinthians 12:17–26)

5. List some of the benefits of team-structured women's ministry.

6. Describe the current structure of your women's ministry team. How many team members do you have? Which positions are filled and which are not?

7. List at least one tip you plan to implement when asking a woman to serve in a leadership role. (See pages 49-53 in *Rethinking Women's Ministry.*)

8. Do you have term limits? If not, explain why you think they are or are not needed in your church.

9. List the documents it would be helpful for each woman on your team to have, such as job descriptions, team covenants, budget information, and room reservation procedures. Place a star beside documents that need to be created.

10. What is your process (or what could it look like) for knowledge transfer and training new leaders?

11. How could your team invite women outside of the team to assist with your women's ministry events and activities? (See page 58 in *Rethinking Women's Ministry*.)

12. Pray and seek what the Lord wants for your team this year. Record how you sense the Lord is leading your team to rethink teams.

Keep a Record

Prayer Requests	PRAYER REQUESTS	BEGAN PRAYING (DATE)	HOW GOD ANSWERED

Action Items	ACTION ITEMS	DATE TO IMPLEMENT	OUTCOME

Sample Job Descriptions

Not all of these positions will be needed for your leadership team. Some of these roles may only need to be filled when you are planning a large-scale event. Other roles may not be necessary due to your women's ministry's purpose or church structure.

Ideally, a leadership team will include at least a Women's Ministry Director, Bible Study Coordinator, Event Coordinator, Social Media Manager, and Service Project Coordinator. (Positions marked * could serve as a team under the Event Coordinator.)

Women's Ministry Director/Leader

- Meets regularly with the pastor who oversees the women's ministry.
- Encourages other team members in their responsibilities, delegates appropriately, and assists when needed.
- Leads women's ministry leadership team meetings, prepares an agenda that encourages the contribution of every team member.
- Identifies training needs for leadership team members and finds opportunities to meet these needs.
- Contacts women's ministry team members as needed and, at a minimum, contacts them on a monthly basis.
- Performs duties of unfilled team positions when necessary.
- Prays regularly for her position, women's ministry team, and the women of the church and community.
- Meets with her successor to ensure a smooth transition.
- Performs other duties as needed.

Treasurer

- Works with women's ministry leader to create a budget for the women's ministry – based on known costs, anticipated expenditures, and expected income. (Adoption of the budget is by the entire leadership team.)
- Reports the financial status at each women's ministry team meeting, identifying shortages and surpluses as appropriate.
- Completes necessary paperwork in accordance with church policies.
- Tracks registrations and payments for events.
- Assists in the distribution of scholarships for women in the group who cannot afford to attend events, ensuring confidentiality for any woman in need.

- Attends to miscellaneous financial matters as needed, including payments to speakers, reimbursement of registration funds, and payments for childcare workers.
- Serves on the leadership team and attends meetings.

Secretary

- Records discussions, decisions, and information shared during leadership team meetings.
- Compiles notes in an organized format.
- Maintains the records of each meeting.
- Distributes minutes from leadership meetings to all team members in a timely manner.
- Serves on the leadership team and attends meetings.

Music & Worship Coordinator *

- Selects music and worship activities that complement the women's ministry event.
- Coordinates the music selections with the event planner.
- Recruits singers and musicians for events.
- Provides lyrics and soundtracks for music as needed.
- Creates PowerPoint slides for lyrics.
- Schedules worship practices prior to events.
- Serves on the leadership team and attends meetings.

Publicity Coordinator *

- Creatively publicizes women's ministry events in the church and community.
- Works with other leadership team members to create event-specific publicity, including registration forms, emails, social media postings, Sunday bulletin announcements, bulletin board displays, brochures, press releases, and other signage.
- Creates and distributes a newsletter on a regular basis.
- Coordinates promotional displays and publicity releases with the church staff.
- Seeks necessary approval on all publicity items per church guidelines.
- Regularly updates the women's ministry page on the church website.
- Serves on the leadership team and attends meetings.

Social Media Manager

- Oversees the selection and usage of social media platforms for the women's ministry.
- Works with the leadership team to create a social media plan and posting guidelines.
- Creates and schedules social media posts.
- Manages social media posting violations per guidelines.
- Serves on the leadership team and attends meetings.

Bible Study Coordinator

- Recruits, trains, and encourages Bible study leaders.
- Maintains regular contact with all Bible study leaders, coaching them through situations as they arise.
- Reviews and purchases Bible study materials.
- Creates a schedule of Bible study classes.
- Works with the publicity coordinator to publicize Bible study offerings.
- Serves on the leadership team and attends meetings.

Service Project Coordinator

- Coordinates prayer efforts for ministry partners, outreach projects, mission trips, and missionaries that are connected to the women's ministry.
- Organizes one-time service project activities for women's ministry events.
- Manages donation collections.
- Works with parachurch ministries to determine future needs and activities.
- Communicates opportunities for service to the women in the church.
- Serves on the leadership team and attends meetings.

Childcare *

- Works with the pastoral staff and leadership to establish policies and procedures for the childcare program if they are not already in place.
- Recruits, trains, and encourages childcare workers, either volunteers or paid help.
- Aids in selecting appropriate materials for each class (lessons, videos, music, toys, etc.).

- Coordinates the setup and takedown of all childcare materials and cleanup.
- Guides the planning of biblical, age-appropriate lessons and schedules for each age group.
- Collects/coordinates supplies, including craft supplies and snacks for each classroom.
- Creates a childcare worker substitute list.
- Ensures that all policies pertaining to childcare at the church are followed.
- Serves on the leadership team and attends meetings.

Decorations *

- Creatively and resourcefully provides decorations for women's ministry events.
- Creates and displays decorations that complement the event theme and purpose.
- Recruits, trains, and encourages the decorations team members.
- Practices good stewardship of decorating funds for events.
- Purchases and maintains a supply of reusable decorative items (vases, candles, mirrors, etc.).
- Serves on the leadership team and attends meetings.

Encouragement

- Organizes meals for women in the church (new baby, illness, death in the family).
- Coordinates encouragement efforts such as sending cards, making phone calls, distributing blessing bags, etc.
- Recruits, trains, and encourages other members of the encouragement team.
- Sends cards in recognition of birthdays and anniversaries of the pastoral staff.
- Serves on the leadership team and attends meetings.

Food (could be combined with Hospitality) *

- Organizes the refreshments at each women's ministry event, delegates responsibilities to team members as needed.
- Oversees or delegates the setting up and refilling of refreshments area and food tables as needed.

- Purchases and maintains a sufficient supply of paper products for women's ministry events.
- Trains and oversees a team that is responsible for setting up and cleaning up the food at each women's ministry event.
- Serves on the leadership team and attends meetings.

Hospitality (could be combined with Food) *

- Focuses on the needs of women and works to create a welcoming atmosphere at each women's ministry event.
- Assures a warm welcome for every woman who comes to women's ministry events.
- Trains and oversees a team of greeters/hostesses for each women's ministry event.
- Serves on the leadership team and attends meetings.

Mentoring/Discipleship

- Oversees the mentoring/discipleship program.
- Recruits, trains, and encourages mentors.
- Prayerfully oversees the pairing of each mentor/mentee.
- Provides guidance to mentors/mentees as needed.
- Shares the praises, needs, and prayer requests of the mentoring program at leadership team meetings.
- Serves on the leadership team and attends meetings.

Women's Ministry Team Needs Assessment

Your input will help us determine where our efforts should be focused during our women's ministry meetings and training this year. We appreciate your honesty and transparency.

Please rate your knowledge or comfort level with the topics below.
1 = Beginner 2 = Intermediate 3 = Expert

Church Procedures

_____ Money matters (reimbursements, requests, collecting money)

_____ Room reservations

_____ Kitchen use (making coffee, cleanup)

_____ Publicity

_____ Registration

Spiritual Growth

_____ Spiritual gifts (understanding and application)

_____ Studying the Bible

_____ Prayer (personal and with others)

_____ Honoring the Sabbath

Relational Skills

_____ Conflict management

_____ Counseling other women

_____ Setting healthy boundaries

_____ Discussion group facilitating

_____ Dealing with gossip

Please note any other area of desired training below:

Women's Ministry Team Covenant

As a member of the women's ministry team:

I will work to fulfill the duties of my role and complete my responsibilities to the best of my ability. If I find I am ever unable to do so, I will immediately notify the women's ministry team director.

I commit to pray for the other women on the team and will build them up with genuine words of encouragement and offer help when appropriate (1 Thessalonians 5:11).

I will follow Matthew 18:15–17 when navigating conflict and disagreements.

I will strive to make my words life giving (Proverbs 18:21).

I will be open to spiritual conversations and learn to share my faith story with others (1 Peter 3:15).

I will prioritize my life, being a good steward of my time, so that women's ministry does not become a burden.

I will be outreach oriented. I will reach out to others during women's ministry events and activities, and I will do my best to recognize the felt needs of women in our group and meet them when appropriate.

I will strive to be a good role model, not behaving in ways that would cause another person to stumble (Romans 14:13, 21).

Name ______________________________

Date ______________

Chapter 5

Rethinking Meetings

1. Read and record **HEBREWS 13:17**.

2. How often does your women's ministry team meet in person? After reading chapter 5 of *Rethinking Women's Ministry*, do you have a reason to suggest or make any changes in how often, when, and where you meet?

3. Does your women's ministry team leader meet regularly with your pastor? What are some benefits of meeting regularly? (See page 67 in *Rethinking Women's Ministry.*)

4. Chapters 4 and 5 of *Rethinking Women's Ministry* are packed with ideas for teams and team meetings. It can be easy to get overwhelmed. God is already doing great things in and through your team. List at least two things your team does well.

5. List at least one thing related to teams or team meetings that you would like to see changed or at least prayerfully considered.

Keep a Record

PRAYER REQUESTS	BEGAN PRAYING (DATE)	HOW GOD ANSWERED	Prayer Requests

ACTION ITEMS	DATE TO IMPLEMENT	OUTCOME	Action Items

Chapter 6

Rethinking Bible Study

1. Read and record **HEBREWS 5:12–14**.

2. Take the Bible Study Health Assessment on page 55. Record here any areas of immediate concern.

3. How does your Bible study schedule provide opportunities for *all* women to attend?

4. **Team task:** If needed, create and implement a survey to clarify your women's availability for Bible study.

5. How might your team address any current childcare struggles?

6. How does your team currently select Bible studies? (See pages 81-83 in *Rethinking Women's Ministry.*) Is there anything you would change about that process?

7. How do you sense God may be directing your team to tweak or even restructure your Bible study format?

8. What ideas for encouraging community outside of the scheduled Bible study class time would you like to see implemented?

9. In what ways might God be asking your team to rethink Bible study?

Keep a Record

Prayer Requests

PRAYER REQUESTS	BEGAN PRAYING (DATE)	HOW GOD ANSWERED

Action Items

ACTION ITEMS	DATE TO IMPLEMENT	OUTCOME

Bible Study Habits Assessment

1. Place an "x" on your level of biblical knowledge according to the scale below.

|———————————————————————————|

Preschooler Elementary School Bible Scholar

2. How often do you read your Bible?

☐ Never ☐ Once a month ☐ 2-3 times a week

☐ Only on Sundays ☐ 2-3 times a month ☐ Almost every day

3. What roadblocks do you face in reading your Bible? (Check all that apply.)

☐ Boring ☐ Don't understand it

☐ Too busy ☐ Struggle to believe it

☐ Not relevant ☐ I don't know where to begin

☐ I don't like to read ☐ Other ____________________

Bible Study Health Assessment

How healthy is your Bible study program?

1. Do the options in your Bible study schedule meet the needs of all of the women in your church?

   ☐ All ☐ Most ☐ Some ☐ None

2. Do you offer childcare for your Bible studies?

   ☐ All ☐ Most ☐ Some ☐ None

3. Do your women regularly read and study the Bible on their own?

   ☐ All ☐ Most ☐ Some ☐ None

4. Do your women understand and apply basic biblical truths?

   ☐ All ☐ Most ☐ Some ☐ None

5. Do your women have an overall understanding of the Bible from start to finish?

   ☐ All ☐ Most ☐ Some ☐ None

6. Does your discussion time challenge and encourage your women to grow spiritually?

   ☐ Yes ☐ No ☐ Probably not; it's rather short

7. Do you provide training for your Bible study group facilitators and teachers?

   ☐ Yes ☐ No ☐ Not sure

8. Do your Bible study groups meet together regularly outside of their scheduled class time?

   ☐ All ☐ Most ☐ Some ☐ None

Discussion Group Guidelines

Discussion groups allow participants to examine topics through the lens of the Bible.

These guidelines will help you to get the most out of your discussion group time:

1. Please keep all sharing confidential.
2. Please do not share anything that might be considered gossip.
3. Be a good listener. Be patient and give others time to process and respond.
4. Be respectful of different perspectives and opinions. Your group members likely have different church experiences and backgrounds, but we are all sisters in Christ. Please refrain from discussing topics (such as politics) or other controversial issues that divide us.
5. Pray for and keep confidential the prayer requests shared in your group.
6. Be willing to be transparent; while at the same time, protect yourself and others by not over-sharing and by limiting details.
7. Stay on topic. Keep your discussion focused on the questions and passage being studied.
8. Refrain from using the names of books, pastors, TV shows, etc., as doing so can be divisive and not biblically accurate. Our focus should be God's Word, not the words of others.

"May the God who gives endurance and encouragement give you the same attitude of mind toward each other that Christ Jesus had, so that with one mind and one voice you may glorify the God and Father of our Lord Jesus Christ." (Romans 15:5–6)

Chapter 7

Rethinking Testimonies and Devotionals

1. Read and record 1 PETER 3:15 and 2 CORINTHIANS 1:3–4.

2. Have you ever publicly shared your testimony (either your salvation story or an experience you've had with Christ)? If not, why?

3. **Challenge:** Complete the "Sharing Your God Story" worksheet at the end of this chapter.

4. When sharing your story, which of the three Cs (current, concise, or Christ-centered) is the biggest struggle for you? Explain why. (See page 95 in *Rethinking Women's Ministry*).

5. **Team task:** Pray and ask God to help you create a list of women to share their stories. Record their names below.

6. Are you and your team members prepared to share the gospel? If not, what will you do to change that? See the list of evangelism tools on page 184 in *Rethinking Women's Ministry* for ideas.

7. After reading chapter 7 in *Rethinking Women's Ministry,* how is God prompting you to rethink the sharing of stories and the gospel at your women's ministry events?

Keep a Record

Prayer Requests	PRAYER REQUESTS	BEGAN PRAYING (DATE)	HOW GOD ANSWERED

Action Items	ACTION ITEMS	DATE TO IMPLEMENT	OUTCOME

Sharing Your God Story

What lesson does God want you to remember and tell others? This worksheet will help you work through the details so you can share your story with others and give God the glory.

1. Think back over the last six months to a year. What have you thanked God for? What did God do for you? Did He redeem, rescue, forgive, or restore you? Did He answer a prayer, change your circumstances, or show His faithfulness in a difficult situation? Did you witness God fulfilling a promise? Write down a brief summary.

2. Now divide that story into three parts. Write a couple of sentences explaining:
   a) How I was
   b) What happened (What did God do?)
   c) How I am now (transformation)

3. To what Bible verse or scripture passage did God point you during this time?

Chapter 8

Rethinking Mentoring and Discipleship

1. Read and record **TITUS 2:3** and **MATTHEW 28:19–20**.

2. Describe your team's current mentoring and discipleship efforts. What do you offer? How many women are involved? What has been the response?

3. What is needed in your church: mentoring, discipleship, or a combination?

4. **Team task:** Create a list of the pros and cons of mentoring and discipleship.

	Organic Mentoring (Informal)	Intentional Mentoring (Formal)	Organic Discipleship (Informal)	Intentional Discipleship (Formal)
PROS				
CONS				

5. What barriers do you see to mentoring and discipling relationships in your church?

6. What can you do to overcome those barriers?

7. How do you sense God may be prompting your team to move forward with a mentoring or discipleship program? If one is already in place, what, if any, changes does your team need to prayerfully consider?

Keep a Record

Prayer Requests

PRAYER REQUESTS	BEGAN PRAYING (DATE)	HOW GOD ANSWERED

Action Items

ACTION ITEMS	DATE TO IMPLEMENT	OUTCOME

Chapter 9

Rethinking Service and Missions

1. Read and record **JAMES 1:22**.

2. List examples of the four levels of missions participation your team has offered in the last ministry year. (See pages 116-117 of *Rethinking Women's Ministry.*)

Levels of Missions Participation	Women's Ministry Events or Activities
Prayer	
Donations	
One-Time Service Projects	
Relationships	

3. Create a list of parachurch ministries your team could prayerfully consider for a future partnership.

4. Create a list of communities in your church neighborhood where God may be calling your women to serve.

5. List any groups of women who regularly come to the church building but don't attend church services or women's ministry activities. (See page 119-120 in *Rethinking Women's Ministry*.)

6. List at least three service project ideas (see pages 121-123 in *Rethinking Women's Ministry*) that you'd like your team to prayerfully consider completing in the next year.

7. In what specific ways do you sense God is prompting your team to rethink service projects and missions opportunities?

Keep a Record

PRAYER REQUESTS	BEGAN PRAYING (DATE)	HOW GOD ANSWERED	Prayer Requests

ACTION ITEMS	DATE TO IMPLEMENT	OUTCOME	Action Items

Chapter 10

Rethinking Your Calendar

1. Read and record **HEBREWS 10:24–25**.

2. How many events do you typically host in one year? Do you feel it's too few, too many, or exactly right?

3. Looking at last year's calendar (or this year if it's already planned), list your events and activities by attendance size. (See page 129 in *Rethinking Women's Ministry.*)

   Large group events:

   Medium-sized events:

   Small group events:

4. Looking at the list you created, what, if any, changes do you think are needed? Remember, "your church size will determine the number of large, medium, and small events you host."[1]

5. **Team task:** Gather and make copies of the calendars from your church and local school system (only those that impact your members). Make a note of other important community events. What are some key events and dates your team needs to plan around?

6. How does your team decide if an event should be canceled? If God is prompting you to reconsider that process, what might need to change?

1 Cyndee Ownbey, *Rethinking Women's Ministry: Biblical, Practical Tools for Cultivating a Flourishing Community* (Charlotte, NC: ONB Press, 2019), 130.

7. What are the benefits of **not** taking a ministry summer sabbatical? (See pages 135-137 in *Rethinking Women's Ministry.*)

8. How do you sense God may be leading your team to rethink your ministry calendar?

Keep a Record

PRAYER REQUESTS	BEGAN PRAYING (DATE)	HOW GOD ANSWERED	Prayer Requests

ACTION ITEMS	DATE TO IMPLEMENT	OUTCOME	Action Items

Chapter 11

Rethinking Women's Ministry Events

1. Read and record **ACTS 2:42**.

2. In the chart below, list the different types of women's ministry events and activities you've offered in the last twelve months. (See pages 142-145 in *Rethinking Women's Ministry*.)

Spiritual Disciplines	Biblical Encouragement	Practical Skills	Service	Fellowship Focused

3. Looking over the completed chart, make a note below of any gaps. Remember, "we're not striving for an equal balance of different women's ministry event types, but we are striving for a variety."[2]

4. In chapter 11 in *Rethinking Women's Ministry* (see page 145), which comments from women about what they do and don't want from women's ministry surprised you or confirmed what you already believed?

5. Is Christ the cornerstone of every event your team offers? If not, how could your team rise to that challenge? (See pages 145-146 in *Rethinking Women's Ministry.*)

2 Cyndee Ownbey, *Rethinking Women's Ministry: Biblical, Practical Tools for Cultivating a Flourishing Community* (Charlotte, NC: ONB Press, 2019), 145.

6. What could your team do to make your events more interactive? List specific ideas that you think will work well with *your* women. (See page 147 in *Rethinking Women's Ministry*.)

7. Have food or door prizes become a burden or focus for your women's ministry events? If so, what changes might you make to keep the focus on Christ?

8. List specific ways in which you can sense God may be leading your team to rethink your women's ministry events.

Keep a Record

PRAYER REQUESTS	BEGAN PRAYING (DATE)	HOW GOD ANSWERED	Prayer Requests

ACTION ITEMS	DATE TO IMPLEMENT	OUTCOME	Action Items

Post-Event Evaluation Form

Briefly describe the event:

Who was your target audience?

What was the purpose/goal of the event?

Describe how attendees encountered Jesus.

How many volunteers were needed to organize it?

Briefly describe your promotion of the event.

What, if any, expenses did you incur in connection with your event? (Itemize if possible.)

Would it be wise to attempt a similar event in the future?

What would you do differently?

What would remain the same?

Briefly describe your impression of how well received your event was by those in attendance.

Chapter 12

Rethinking Publicity

1. Read and record **MATTHEW 13:16**.

2. Do women of all ages and stages in your church *really* know they are invited to women's ministry events and activities? Explain your answer.

3. If your women's ministry has a name, does it require an explanation? Consider whether or not a newcomer would know an event is for all women.

4. Make a list of the methods your team currently uses to publicize women's ministry events. Are there any additional ideas from chapter 12 in *Rethinking Women's Ministry* that you think you should add or try?

5. **Team task:** Survey your women to discover which social media platforms they engage with regularly. List them below.

6. Place a check beside each of the online publicity tools your team currently utilizes. Note: you don't need to use them all, but you should have an online presence.

_____ Email list
_____ Web page on the church website
_____ Facebook page
_____ Closed Facebook group
_____ Instagram account
_____ Other ______________________________

7. What additions or changes to your online presence should your team prayerfully consider?

8. In what ways is God leading you to rethink publicity?

Keep a Record

Prayer Requests

PRAYER REQUESTS	BEGAN PRAYING (DATE)	HOW GOD ANSWERED

Action Items

ACTION ITEMS	DATE TO IMPLEMENT	OUTCOME

Publicity Form

Event name:	
Event date:	Cost:
What participants need to bring:	
Event contact person (name, number, and email):	
Registration information (how and when):	
Childcare information:	
Hook or tagline:	
Publicity strategy: ☐ Sunday bulletin ☐ Special bulletin insert ☐ Church newsletter ☐ Church Facebook page ☐ Church website ☐ Facebook group ☐ Mailer ☐ Email	☐ Sunday morning PowerPoint ☐ Flyer in bathroom stalls ☐ Flyers on bulletin boards ☐ Sunday school announcements ☐ Newspapers ☐ Radio stations ☐ Social media ☐ Other________________
Logo needed (ministry, church, event):	
Graphic(s) needed:	
Date to begin publicity:	
Main text for publicity:	

Chapter 13

Making Changes and Managing Sacred Cows

1. Read and record **ISAIAH 43:18–19**.

2. Make a list of women's ministry practices, events, and activities in your church that could be considered sacred cows. If you're stuck, consider what would cause an outcry if your team stopped doing it.

3. Prayerfully review each event and activity from the last twelve months. Identify which should be refined or removed and which should remain.

Event/Activity	Refine	Remove	Remain	Justification

Event/Activity	Refine	Remove	Remain	Justification

4. **Team task:** Select one event or activity that has been identified as needing refinement. Make a list of the elements that should stay the same and which should be altered. Consider the target audience, publicity materials, event schedule, speaker(s), day, time, length, location, and purpose. (See page 172 in *Rethinking Women's Ministry.*)

   Remember, it's often best to make small changes over time. Place a star beside the items you think should be addressed this year.

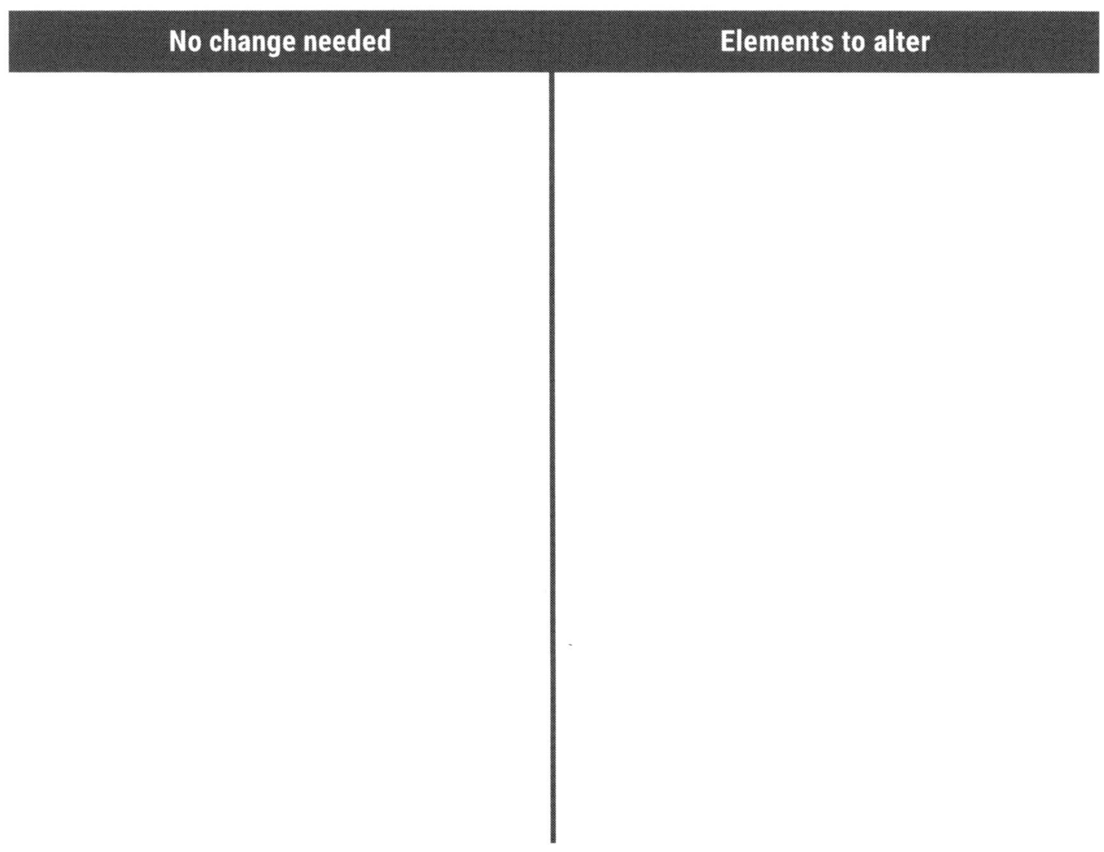

No change needed	Elements to alter

5. How do you sense God is prompting your team to respond to sacred cows?

Keep a Record

PRAYER REQUESTS	BEGAN PRAYING (DATE)	HOW GOD ANSWERED	
			Prayer Requests

ACTION ITEMS	DATE TO IMPLEMENT	OUTCOME	
			Action Items

Women's Ministry Health Assessment

First, answer the questions. Be specific. Your answers should reflect how and why, not just a yes or no. Then rate each area on a scale from 1 to 10.

1 = None/Lacking greatly
5 = Fair/Some
10 = Off the charts/No need for improvement

1. **Spiritual Growth** – Health Rating _____

   Describe several examples of unbelievers who have come into a relationship with Christ through your ministry. If you can't think of any, how often do you think this happens in your ministry? Describe examples of how women are engaging in discipleship and growing spiritually. If you can't think of any, what would it look like if you did observe this in your ministry? List examples of how women are increasingly spending time in prayer, God's Word, and service.

2. **Reputation** – Health Rating _____

   How would you describe the overall sentiment toward the women's ministry in your church? What is your ministry's reputation? Ask some women outside of your leadership team. Ask the pastoral staff. Are you viewed as a clique? Exclusive? Welcoming? Warm?

3. **Leadership** – Health Rating _____

   List several examples of ways you are developing new leaders. Describe your plan to seek out and develop leaders among the women in your church. List examples that show whether you have the same core group of women who lead everything or whether you are open to new faces in your leadership circle.

4. **Volunteers** – Health Rating _____

   How would you describe the strength of your volunteer teams? What type of response do you receive when you ask for volunteers? Describe the attitude of your volunteers. Are your volunteers compassionate and committed or weary and stale?

5. **Turnout** - Health Rating _____

   What do your numbers tell you? Make a list of events that have a strong, solid turnout and those events and activities that are struggling. Keep in mind that a strong turnout is not an equivalent to a gold star from God. Some of the best-attended events can be lacking in direction or mission.

6. **Mission** - Health Rating _____

   What is the focus of your women's ministry? Describe how your women's ministry fulfills its mission or purpose. Explain how your church would be at a loss if your women's ministry ceased to exist.

7. **Outreach** - Health Rating _____

   List ways in which your events and activities include women from outside of the church. Explain how your team utilizes the women's ministry as a bridge, encouraging women to attend worship and serve as part of the church body.

Add up your health scores and see where you fall in the chart below.

Scores	Assessment
55-70	Congratulations, your ministry is healthy! If you haven't asked your pastoral staff to complete the assessment, please consider doing so to make certain you haven't missed any signs or symptoms that need attention.
30-54	Looks like your ministry is in fair to good health. Where can you make some changes to push your ministry into the healthy zone? Be quick to address areas that rated a 4 or lower.
15-29	We need to make a consult with the Great Physician. It appears you may be struggling with some chronic issues. Let's nip things in the bud and create a plan to address areas that scored below a 4. You may want to tackle a different area each month at your team meeting.
0-14	Your ministry is showing signs and symptoms that need to be addressed immediately. Work together to come up with a plan to address the most chronic needs first. God is in the restoration business; let's pray and seek wise counsel to restore your ministry's health.

This exercise is not designed to make you or your team feel bad but to shine a light on areas of your ministry that need some extra attention and to celebrate those areas in which your team excels.

Let's celebrate what we do well and embrace the growth opportunities that God has revealed. None of us is perfect, and I don't expect any ministry to score a 70.

It's easy for us to lose sight of the greater picture in the midst of planning events and activities. We can become so focused on our women having fun that we miss opportunities to encourage spiritual growth, discipleship, and service.

Take this opportunity to see the bigger picture and fuel change where it is needed. Consider making this assessment an annual process, always working toward creating a healthier ministry.

SECTION 2

Bonus Chapter and Worksheet

Bonus Chapter

Rethinking Technology and Communication

"Therefore encourage one another and build each other up, just as in fact you are doing."
—1 Thessalonians 5:11

AS MANY LEADERS LEARNED DURING THE coronavirus quarantine in the spring of 2020, technology provides the opportunity for us to encourage one another when we can't meet together. As in-person gatherings were canceled, women's ministry teams and Bible study leaders scrambled to learn how to use technology to transition from in-person ministry to online ministry. Their efforts paid off as Bible studies continued via Zoom, prayer meetings were held over conference calls, and women gathered virtually for coffee and conversation.

While virtual meetups will certainly never replace in-real-life community, the ability to continue Bible study meetings and meet virtually had many benefits. Teams that chose to transition to virtual women's ministry saw their efforts bear fruit as women continued to grow spiritually and in relationship with one another. Transitioning meetings to online also provided comfort and a sense of normalcy as we simultaneously shared our struggles and studied God's Word.

I pray that the new tools we've learned to use won't be thrown by the wayside when large group gatherings resume. (As I write this chapter, we're still facing at least two more weeks of stay-at-home quarantine orders.) The connections that we've nurtured online will no doubt flourish when we gather in real life. Yet, there is no reason why we shouldn't continue to connect online in between our women's ministry events to offer regular support and encouragement.

In this bonus chapter, I want to challenge you to prayerfully assess your approach to technology. God may prompt your team to use technology in new ways to cultivate community and create connection. Your team may decide to add another technology tool to your arsenal. I pray that He'll reveal how your team can best use technology to connect and communicate with each other and with Christ.

In this chapter, we'll look at which technology tools your team may want to use. We'll also focus on how to increase engagement and create opportunities for connection.

Technology provides the opportunity for us to encourage one another when we can't meet together.

While you may already be using technology to publicize your women's ministry events, we want to move beyond communicating information **to** your women toward communicating **with** your women. We can continue conversations and deepen connections until we meet again in person.

Email Lists

Email lists allow your team to make direct contact with virtually every woman in your church to communicate important information. Hopefully your church has an email program that you can access and utilize to communicate with the women that attend your women's ministry events. If not, take a look at using a free or inexpensive email list service such as Mailchimp or MailerLite. I do not recommend using a personal email account.

What are the benefits of using an email list service?

1. **Access** - One of the most significant benefits of using an email list service is shared access with women's ministry team members. If only one person has all of the email addresses on their personal computer, you and the rest of your team must rely on that person's availability and ability to send out your information correctly and promptly.
2. **Delivery** – Not sure if your women received your email? Now you can check. Most services provide detailed reports that allow you to see who opened each email and who did not. You may even be able to re-send your email to those that didn't open it the first time.
3. **Ease** – You can easily add new women to the email list.
4. **Replies** – You eliminate the ability of your women to "reply all," sending spam or personal information to the entire group.
5. **Security** – Your women's ministry email address book is stored securely online. It isn't lost if someone's laptop crashes or is infected by a computer virus.
6. **Templates** – Most email list services allow you to create templates so all of your emails have a similar look and style. Links to social media and your website can be embedded at the bottom of each email. There's no

need to create a pretty PDF or send plain text – you can customize your emails, and they'll look professional and impressive!

Email is the best way to communicate important information to your women. While not all of your women may be active on social media, almost all of them have an email address. Algorithms and lengthy newsfeeds mean we can't guarantee every woman will see every social media post.

Social Media

Social media, unlike email, can be interactive. With so many different social media options available and new ones popping up regularly, you may be unsure about where to start. How can your team determine which social media channel will be most effective for your ministry?

The quickest and easiest way to figure out which social media channel your team should focus on (start with one) is to ask your women which social media channels they use regularly. This is one of those times where the majority should rule. Go where most of your women already spend their time. Most likely, that will be Facebook.

I recommend setting up a private Facebook group rather than a Facebook page for your women's ministry. Groups provide a level of community and confidentiality that your women will appreciate. Pages talk to your audience, while groups encourage conversation with your audience. Remember: discussion, not lecture.

Determine the purpose of your social media account and put it in writing.

You may be surprised by the connections and community that can occur inside a private Facebook group. One leader shared with me the snowball effect that a simple icebreaker question had inside their Facebook group. Their social media manager posted a question asking, "What is your favorite restaurant for eating lunch?" The recommendations poured in, and then women started making plans in the comments to meet for lunch!

You or your team members may dread the thought of using social media for your women's ministry. I understand. Social media can be the source of a lot of drama and negativity. You may even debate the wisdom in asking women to spend more time on their devices. To keep your social media account from becoming a source of division or distraction, your team will need to set some guidelines.

How to avoid social media pitfalls:

1. Determine the purpose of your social media account and put it in writing. Share the purpose in your account's description so new members understand your focus.
2. Create posting and group guidelines. What should be posted? What types of posts won't be permitted? Being proactive and not reactive

will benefit everyone. Take into consideration political posts, self-promotion, videos, quotes, articles that may differ theologically from your church's beliefs, prayer requests, complaints, etc. Outline a plan for dealing with post violations.

3. Recruit someone to serve as your social media manager. They should also serve as a member of the women's ministry leadership team. Having someone committed to overseeing and scheduling your social media posts will provide the consistency needed to encourage engagement. This person should also address violations to your posting guidelines immediately and consistently.

Lack of engagement is one of the frustrations that leaders often encounter in setting up a social media account. I've found that if leaders take the time to coach and cheer their group members, they'll see an increase in engagement.

Coach + Cheer = Engagement

Here are four suggestions to encourage engagement:

1. Set up a welcome sequence. Create a series of two to three posts that invite women to comment and provide a warm welcome to your group. This gets them in the habit of responding to posts. You could ask them to share: What is your favorite restaurant or type of food to eat? What is one Bible verse you treasure? What is one of your favorite things to do for fun?
2. Prime the pump. Ask your women's ministry team members to comment on and like the posts. Sometimes women are waiting for someone else to go first. Your team is also modeling the activity that you desire.
3. Respond to comments as you are able. While your social media manager may not be able to respond to every single comment, it takes mere moments to hit the "like" button. The more you interact and respond to comments, the more your women will comment and reply.
4. Set up a social media calendar. Aim to post once a day but vary the types of things you post (see below for examples). Consistency will encourage engagement.

Creating an active online community takes time. Be patient and continue to coach and cheer your women. Expect interaction to ebb and flow. You may feel as if you're throwing spaghetti at a wall hoping something will stick. Keep at it; something will stick!

What should you post on your social media channel?

1. Bible verse graphics – Consider sharing the context of the verse.
2. Inspirational quotes – Make certain any quote you share from someone, living or dead, lines up with the beliefs of your church. To avoid any

issues that might arise if an author, speaker, or pastor changes their theological positions, you may wish to quote only famous Christian people who have died.

3. Event publicity – Share event information, including registration deadlines, speaker photos, registration links, donation collections, sneak peek photos, teasers, childcare signup, etc.
4. Request feedback – The polling features on social media can provide instant feedback to help your team make decisions and plans. Use polls just for fun too! Examples: Do you prefer coffee or tea? Beach or mountains?
5. Share short teachings or personal stories – Consider asking specific women in your church to write a short teaching or story. Reach out to women in your church who are speakers and authors; they may be willing to help.
6. Memes – Add a bit of humor to your social media feed with photos or graphics.
7. Links to biblically sound resources – Check with your church staff for a list of recommended authors and websites.
8. Photos – Share images from past events and for upcoming events.
9. Videos – Share highlights from a past event, create a promo video for an upcoming event, record and share testimonies, and interview team members or women in your church. Shorter is better; break up long videos into multiple videos.
10. Icebreaker questions – Consider using a mix of fun and faith-focused questions. Icebreakers encourage interaction and provide connection opportunities.
11. Worship videos – Share links to music videos that Christian artists have posted on YouTube or Vimeo.
12. Spotify song lists – Create and share a song list for your event or a list of inspirational songs.
13. Prayer prompts – Invite your women to join your team in praying for specific groups of people, missionaries, or topics.
14. Ministry updates – Share testimonials from a recent event or activity. Encourage registration by announcing the shrinking number of remaining retreat tickets.

Icebreakers encourage interaction and provide connection opportunities.

You've no doubt encountered social media posts that are not helpful and are inaccurate and unbiblical. I suggest you avoid these:

1. Quotes, videos, or posts that do not align with your church's beliefs
2. Bible verses that are taken out of context

3. Anything that shames a group of people (child- or parent-bashing memes, for example)
4. Content that violates your church's social media guidelines
5. Content unrelated to your purpose

Using a social media schedule will keep your social media manager and your women from being overwhelmed. I suggest creating a weekly plan with one post each day. Decide what type of post (from those listed above) you want to create or share each day of the week. Here's a sample schedule to get your wheels turning.

Saturday – icebreaker question
Sunday – Bible verse
Monday – a link to a blog post focused on faith or spiritual growth
Tuesday – inspirational quote
Wednesday – prayer requests and praises
Thursday – photo from a past event or publicity for an upcoming event
Friday – something fun like a meme

Having a written weekly schedule will simplify the process and minimize the time needed to schedule posts and help you keep the focus on Christ. You can always change up the types of posts to communicate important event information or point women toward time-sensitive resources.

Texting

Texting is another way to use technology to communicate with your women. First, check with your church staff to see if there's a tool you can use before setting up something new. Decide as a team what information will be distributed via text and how often texts will be sent out.

Many women strongly dislike being added to a group chat without permission, so be sure to send individual texts if your group or list is small enough; otherwise, use a texting app. As with all technology initiatives, give women the opportunity to sign up or opt out. Remind, SlickText, Text2Group Pro, GroupMe, Reach, Flocknote, and Text in Church are some of the programs leaders use to text their women.

Websites

A dedicated women's ministry page on your church website provides women the chance to check out your ministry before attending, so be sure to include information and photos that will appeal to guests. Consider setting up a separate web page for events that require registration and then share direct links to that page on social media. A web page is also a great place to publicize your ministry's mission statement, logo, and scripture focus for the year. Outdated ministry information on your church website is a big turnoff, so don't overlook the importance of regularly updating your website information.

Blog posts used to be quite popular on church and ministry websites. However, staff members and volunteers soon grew tired of the time needed to write, edit, publish, and publicize each post. If your team feels led to share regular blog posts, sharing a shorter version of the content on Facebook or Instagram will yield more views and interaction.

Video Conferencing

During the quarantine, Zoom and other video conferencing tools became the go-to technology tool for many churches and ministries. Leaders found that seeing one another provided connection in ways that responding to Facebook posts did not.

Video conferencing can still be a useful tool for women's ministry. If a women's ministry team member is unable to attend your team meeting because she is under the weather or caring for a sick child, she may be able to participate via video.

Even if your team offers daytime and evening Bible study options, there may be a small group of women who are unable to attend due to extenuating circumstances. Your team may want to offer a weekly video conference call so those women can still participate in an online study through your church rather than seeking outside resources.

Learning how to use technology can be time consuming and even at times frustrating, but it's worth the work to nurture relationships when we're not meeting together in person. Just as plants without water will wither, so will relationships; they are more likely to flourish if there is regular and consistent communication and interaction. Social media can fill the need for connection between your women's ministry meetings. You may even find that your attendance increases as women look forward to connecting in person.

Prayer

God, give us wisdom in how we can best use technology to encourage connections and communicate with our women. Help us to use technology in a way that encourages our women to grow closer to one another and to You. Amen.

PRAYER POINTS: WHAT IS GOD PROMPTING ME TO MAKE A MATTER OF PRAYER?

PP

ACTION ITEMS: LIST THOSE THINGS UPON WHICH YOU SENSE GOD IS PROMPTING YOU TO TAKE ACTION.

AI

Rethinking Technology and Communication

1. Read and record **JOHN 13:34–35** and **1 THESSALONIANS 5:11**.

2. Which social media platforms does your ministry currently use?

3. What is the purpose of each of your social media accounts?

4. Create a sample weekly social media schedule.

Sunday	
Monday	
Tuesday	
Wednesday	
Thursday	
Friday	
Saturday	

5. Which technology tools do you sense God wants your team to use to nurture connection and increase communication?

Keep a Record

PRAYER REQUESTS	BEGAN PRAYING (DATE)	HOW GOD ANSWERED	Prayer Requests

ACTION ITEMS	DATE TO IMPLEMENT	OUTCOME	Action Items

SECTION 3

Summarize Your Discoveries

As you've worked through the worksheets, you've likely uncovered many things your ministry should continue to do. You've also probably decided there are a few things your team should start to do and some you may want to stop doing. You may find it helpful to make a list of each of those thoughts on the next few pages. I would suggest working through these questions on your own and then together with your team, if you have one.

Pray over the items on each list and ask God to reveal which ones your team should move forward on now and which ones should wait. As you discuss your answers, I pray that God will confirm as well as change your responses in accordance with His will for your ministry.

1. **Reflect:** What do you think God is asking our women's ministry to start doing that we are not doing?

2. What do you sense God is bringing to an end or asking us to stop doing?

3. What is our women's ministry team doing that you sense that God wants us to continue doing?

SECTION 4

Bonus Resources

Icebreaker Questions

The following 125 icebreaker questions are for your team to use on social media, to encourage connection in your small group, or as an activity at a women's ministry event.

Ideas for how to use the questions at an event or meeting:

1. Print the questions on strips of paper and ask each person to draw one out of a bag, bucket, or hat.
2. Match questions to candy colors. Place a bowl in the center of the table, and whichever color a person chooses first is the question they have to answer.
3. Match each question to a number on a die and have participants roll and answer the corresponding question.
4. Print the icebreaker questions on cards and randomly place them at each place setting.
5. Select one question for the entire group to answer. Have everyone write their answer on an index card and then invite the group to guess which answer belongs to which person.
6. Select one question and have everyone in the circle or at the table share their answer.
7. Place two icebreaker questions on each slip of paper so participants can choose which question they want to answer.
8. Cover a beach ball with icebreaker questions. Throw the ball and have participants answer the question that lands underneath one hand when they catch it.

Ideas for how to use the questions on social media:

1. Ask the question on your Facebook page or in your Facebook group.
2. Create a graphic that features the question.
3. Use a related photograph or image to draw attention to the question.
4. Ask the question in your Instagram or Facebook stories.
5. Film a short video and ask the question verbally. This could be a fun way for women to get to know each other if you include a short introduction. For example, *"Hi, I'm Cyndee Ownbey, and I serve as a Bible study facilitator on Wednesday mornings. Today we'd like to know, 'What is your favorite time of the day and why?' Please share your answer in the comments below."*

I've broken the following icebreakers into two categories: general and faith-focused. General icebreakers are great for warming up a group because they invite women to share their opinions or reveal information about their personal preferences and experiences, which provide opportunities for connection.

Asking women to share something deep and personal with women they may have just met or don't know well can be awkward. You'll want to save most of the faith-focused icebreaker questions for groups that know each other.

General Icebreaker Questions

1. What is your favorite time of the day and why?
2. What was the best job you've ever had?
3. What was the worst job you've ever had?
4. What is the best vacation you've ever taken?
5. What is the most recent movie/book that you've seen/read?
6. What is your favorite town/city in the world? Why?
7. What are three things you do in the morning after you get out of bed?
8. How do you like to spend a rainy day?
9. If you could replay a fun (or deep or big) moment in your life, what would you choose?
10. What would be a perfect afternoon for you?
11. If you were mayor for the day, what three things would you change about your city?
12. What is your favorite smell? Why do you like it?
13. What is the weirdest thing you have ever eaten?
14. If you could eliminate one thing from your daily schedule, what would it be and why?
15. Tell us something you hate doing. Why?
16. What is your pet peeve?
17. What is the one thing (besides Jesus and your Bible) you can't live without?
18. As a child, what did you want to be when you grew up?
19. What do you consider to be the most valuable thing you owned when you were a teenager?
20. What was your best subject in school?
21. What was your worst subject in school?

22. If you were to perform in the circus, what would you do?
23. If you could have had the starring role in one film that was already made, which movie would you pick?
24. What is your favorite song?
25. When trick-or-treating as a kid, was there any kind of candy that you didn't like to get?
26. If you had one extra hour of free time a day, how would you use it?
27. What was your favorite TV show when you were growing up?
28. Name the most famous person you've had a face-to-face encounter with.
29. If you won a million dollars, what would you do with it?
30. What was your nickname growing up (or now)?
31. Who was your favorite teacher and why?
32. If you knew you could not fail, what would you do?
33. What was your favorite thing to play with as a child?
34. If you could rid the world of one thing, what would it be?
35. If you could be invisible for a day, what would you do?
36. What is your favorite ice cream flavor?
37. If someone rented a billboard for you, what would you put on it?
38. What is your favorite holiday?
39. Which member of your family has had the greatest influence on you?
40. What is your favorite dessert?
41. What is something you have that is of sentimental value?
42. What one modern convenience could you not live without?
43. If you could meet anyone from history, who would you meet and why?
44. What is your favorite podcast?
45. Where would you like to retire and why?
46. What is your favorite season?
47. Which of Snow White's seven dwarfs describes you best and why? (Doc, Happy, Bashful, Sleepy, Sneezy, Grumpy, Dopey)
48. If you had unlimited money and space, what one thing would you add to your house?

49. If you could go only to one restaurant for the next five years, which would it be?
50. What is your favorite breakfast?
51. If you had to describe your day as a traffic sign, what would it be?
52. What is your favorite part of your day?
53. What time period from the past would you most have liked to live in and why?
54. Describe your past week as a weather forecast.
55. If you could travel anywhere in the world, where would you go?
56. If you had to lose one of your five senses, which one of them would you prefer to lose and why?
57. Name one important characteristic you look for in a friend.
58. If you could be any superhero, which one would you be and why?
59. What are your favorite pizza toppings?
60. What is your favorite candy bar?
61. If you had to give up one food that you like forever, what would it be?
62. What is your favorite board game or card game?
63. What is your favorite winter activity?
64. What is your favorite summer activity?
65. What is your favorite fall activity?
66. What is your favorite spring activity?
67. What is the oldest piece of clothing you still own and wear?
68. If you could choose any view in the world to be visible from your bed, what would it be?
69. What is the best gift anyone has ever given to you?
70. What TV game show, past or present, would you want to go on?
71. What is your favorite Disney movie?
72. If you could give one sentence of advice about how to live life, what would it be?
73. What is your favorite tradition?
74. If you had to wear a t-shirt with one word on it for the rest of your life, what word would you choose?
75. What is your favorite kind of cookie?

Faith-Focused Icebreaker Questions

1. If Jesus joined you for breakfast, what would you talk about?
2. What is your favorite Bible verse?
3. What person from the Bible would you most like to meet and why?
4. If you could insert yourself into any story from the Bible, which would you choose?
5. What is one book of the Bible you would like to learn more about?
6. Which person from the Bible do you most admire and why?
7. What is your favorite book of the Bible?
8. If you could add an eleventh commandment to the Ten Commandments, what would it be?
9. When did Jesus first become real to you?
10. If you could spend the day with anyone from the Bible, who would you choose?
11. What is your ideal Bible study location or situation?
12. If you could have any one prayer answered, what would it be?
13. If you could take a mission trip anywhere in the world, where would you choose to go?
14. Name a book from the Bible that has changed your life.
15. If you could have coffee (or tea) with one person from the Bible other than Jesus, who would you choose and why?
16. Describe your personal Bible study time using only emojis.
17. What is one Bible verse that gives you comfort in difficult times?
18. Would you rather read the whole Bible in a year or dig deep into just a few books of the Bible?
19. Share a link to one of your favorite worship songs.
20. What biblical event would you like to witness if you could?
21. Which person in the Bible do you most relate to and why?
22. If you could ask God one question, what would you ask?
23. What is your favorite Christian movie?
24. What is your favorite hymn?
25. How have you seen someone serve others in the last month?

26. Who is one person in the Bible you would like to learn more about?
27. Share a tip for memorizing Bible verses.
28. Share a Bible study tip for busy women.
29. Where is your favorite place to pray?
30. Where do you feel closest to God?
31. If you could take a spiritual retreat, where would you like to go?
32. Who has had a significant influence on your Christian life and how?
33. What is one thing you enjoy about our church?
34. What have you learned recently about the Bible or God?
35. What has another person done to encourage your spiritual growth?
36. How have you seen someone love like Jesus in the past week?
37. What is something you struggle to be a good steward of?
38. What is something you are currently praying about?
39. Which fruit of the spirit do you find challenging?
40. Would you rather celebrate Easter or Christmas?
41. What is one of your favorite Easter songs?
42. What is one of your favorite Christmas songs?
43. Besides attending church, what is one of your Easter traditions?
44. Besides attending church, what is one of your Christmas traditions?
45. Which member of your family has had the greatest influence on your faith?
46. How do you keep record of answered prayers?
47. Share a tip for praying for others.
48. What is one prayer request that you've seen God answer in the last year?
49. What was your favorite women's ministry event this year?
50. What is one thing you wish every person knew about God?

Leadership Retreat Sample Schedules

You'll find several detailed leadership retreat options in these next few pages. I pray that the Lord will show you which option is best for your team and He will guide you to make any adjustments that would benefit your group.

As you work to plan your Rethinking Women's Ministry Retreat, you'll need decide on these items:

1. Which parts of the book you want to discuss
2. What chapters you want your team to read in advance
3. Which workbook pages you want the team to complete in advance
4. Which workbook pages you might want to do together as a whole group or in small groups at your retreat
5. Which bonus materials you wish to use at your retreat
6. How you'll form an action plan
7. Who will lead each session
8. How you'll address issues going forward
9. How you'll continue the discussion if your team needs additional time

Option #1: Half-day, 4 hours

Purchase a copy of the *Rethinking Women's Ministry* book and workbook for each team member two to three months before your leadership retreat. Ask each member to complete the book and workbook pages on their own.

Begin the meeting with a time of prayer.

Remind the team of your women's ministry mission statement, purpose, and vision (you may not have or need all three).

Schedule approximately one hour to work through each one of the Summarize Your Discoveries questions on page 121. (You may want to ask your team members to complete them before you meet so your time can be spent discussing everyone's answers.)

Pray and ask God to help your team determine which items should be addressed in the next three months. If time allows, formulate a plan for taking action.

Option #2: Half-day, 4 hours

Purchase a copy of the *Rethinking Women's Ministry* book and workbook for each team member at least a month before your leadership retreat.

Decide in advance which chapters you want your team to focus on. The Ministry Health Assessment may be helpful. Ask each member to read and complete the workbook pages for those specific chapters.

Begin the meeting with a time of prayer.

Discuss those specific chapters and the corresponding answers to the workbook pages during your time together.

Option # 3: Two-day retreat

Day 1

Prayer
Icebreaker game
Select two chapters to discuss and review worksheet answer
Worship

Day 2: Morning

Prayer
Worship
Testimony
Select two chapters to discuss (approx. 1 hour each)

Day 2: Afternoon

Icebreaker
Select two chapters to discuss
Complete the questions in Summarize Your Discoveries
Prayer

Option #4: Two-day retreat

Divide book and worksheet chapters by team roles. Ask each team leader to read the corresponding chapter, complete the worksheets, and report their discoveries to the group.

You may wish to leave time for group discussion at the end of each team member's presentation.

Add time for prayer and worship before or after each group of presentations.

Printable Bonus Materials

You'll find the worksheets, forms, and assessments mentioned throughout *Rethinking Women's Ministry Workbook* available as a free downloadable PDF at **www.rethinkingwomensministry.com**.

- 31 Introduction Icebreaker Questions
- Bible Study Habits
- Discussion Group Guidelines
- Post-Event Evaluation Form
- Publicity Form
- Sample Job Descriptions
- Sharing Your God Story
- Women's Ministry Health Assessment
- Women's Ministry Team Covenant
- Women's Ministry Team Needs Assessment

About the Author

Cyndee Ownbey is the author of *Rethinking Women's Ministry: Biblical, Practical Tools for Cultivating a Flourishing Community.* Cyndee serves as a mentor to thousands of women's ministry leaders through her website and Facebook community, Women's Ministry Toolbox. Pulling from twenty years of experience with ministering to women, Cyndee shares tried-and-true women's ministry tips and ideas while pointing leaders toward God and the Holy Word. Service in women's ministries in five different churches has enabled Cyndee to relate to a variety of ministry situations and challenges.

Over the years, God has expanded the reach of Women's Ministry Toolbox to include a Facebook group of over 4000 women's ministry leaders, an online classroom featuring women's ministry training, and several printable women's ministry resources. In the fall of 2019, Cyndee hosted the first Gather and Glean Women's Ministry Training and Retreat for leaders to gather and glean inspiration from one another.

Cyndee's resources for leaders include:

- READ Bible Study Workbook and Group Kit
- Prayer Warrior Boot Camp Online Course and Group Kit
- Bible Study Facilitator Training Online Course
- Women's Ministry Event Planning Online Course
- How to Select a Bible Study for Your Group Online Course
- *Women's Ministry Binder Essentials* eBook
- *Everything You Need to Know About Planning a Retreat* eBook
- *12 Days of Christmas Icebreaker Games* eBook

For more information visit **womensministrytoolbox.com/resources**.

Cyndee enjoys training women's ministry leaders and teaching at women's events and conferences when the opportunity allows.

When she isn't serving in the church as a Bible study leader or encouraging leaders online, you'll likely find Cyndee curled up with a good book. Cyndee and her husband enjoy cheering for the Tarheels and spending time with their sons at the beach.

You can find her on Facebook, Instagram, and Pinterest **@womensministrytoolbox** and online at **www.womensministrytoolbox.com**.

Rethinking Women's Ministry invites leaders to take a fresh look at their women's ministry framework through the lens of Scripture and prayer. Cyndee tackles the common obstacles women's ministry leaders face: generational gaps, unwilling mentors, biblical illiteracy, cliques, social media, sacred cows, and more!

Using real-life, practical examples and easy-to-adopt strategies, *Rethinking Women's Ministry* gives leaders tools to develop a women's ministry that flourishes!

Find the tools you need to:

- Expand the reach of your ministry
- Adapt to today's culture
- Engage women of all generations
- Nurture transformation with grace
- Effectively evaluate your ministry and events

With a vision for women's ministry in the modern church, Cyndee challenges leaders to rethink current ministry practices. Rather than focusing on Pinterest-worthy productions, this book urges leaders to design events and activities that grow meaningful connections with one another and cultivate a deeper relationship with God – the elements of true discipleship.

www.rethinkingwomensministry.com

Made in the USA
Monee, IL
15 March 2023

29919782R00077